REPTILES

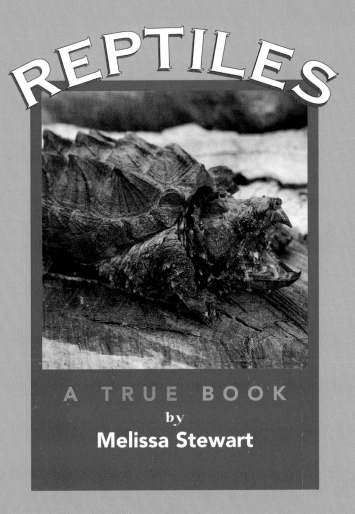

A TRUE BOOK

by

Melissa Stewart

Children's Press®
A Division of Grolier Publishing

New York London Hong Kong Sydney
Danbury, Connecticut

An Arabian cobra

Content Consultants
Jan Jenner, Ph.D.
Jim Van Abbema, Ph.D.

The photograph on the cover shows a humphead forest dragon. The photograph on the title page shows an alligator snapping turtle.

Visit Children's Press® on the Internet at:
http://publishing.grolier.com

Library of Congress Cataloging-in-Publication Data

Stewart, Melissa.
    Reptiles / by Melissa Stewart.
       p. cm. — (A true book)
    Includes bibliographical references and index.
    Summary: Describes the basic behavior, physical traits, and life cycles of reptiles.
    ISBN: 0-516-22036-5 (lib. bdg.)   0-516-25953-9 (pbk.)
    1. Reptiles—Juvenile literature. [1. Reptiles.] I. Title. II. Series.
QL644.2.S746 2001
597.9—dc21   99-057897

©2001 Children's Press®,
A Division of Grolier Publishing Co., Inc.
All rights reserved. Published simultaneously in Canada.
Printed in the United States of America.
1 2 3 4 5 6 7 8 9 10 R 10 09 08 07 06 05 04 03 02 01

Contents

This gaboon viper flicks its tongue to smell (above). The red-bellied turtle often rests for hours on logs (right). Nile crocodiles sometimes eat humans, but this one is eating an impala (below).

What Is a Reptile?

A snake flicks its long tongue as it slithers along the ground. A turtle sits on a rotting log and basks in the sun. A crocodile grabs a fish with its mighty jaws. These are the images that come to mind when someone says the word "reptile."

Have you ever wondered what makes reptiles different from other groups of animals? All reptiles have three things in common—scaly skin, lungs, and a backbone. Most young reptiles hatch from tough, leathery eggs laid on land and look like smaller versions of their parents.

A reptile's scales protect it from enemies and help keep its insides moist. The scales of most snakes feel smooth, but

When sand lizards hatch from their leathery eggs, they are tiny—about 1.5 inches (4 centimeters) long.

most lizards have rough, spiky scales. The scales of a crocodile are hardened with bone. A turtle's scales cover a hard, bony shell.

Reptiles breathe air with their lungs. A reptile's backbone does the same job as your backbone. It supports the animal's body and helps it move.

A reptile is cold blooded. It controls its body temperature by moving in and out of the sun. At night, a reptile's body cools down, and all its body systems work slowly.

Each morning, a reptile warms itself in the sun. When the animal is warm, its body

While cooling down underneath a bush, this leopard lizard is also well hidden from its enemies.

works faster. A snake can dart out to catch a mouse, and a lizard can run along the ground at top speed. By noon, a reptile may start to get too hot. To cool down, it hides in a shady place.

Groups of Reptiles

Millions of years ago, a group of reptiles called dinosaurs ruled the planet. They were the largest and most dangerous animals on land, in the water, and in the air. There are no dinosaurs alive today, but there are still plenty of reptiles. Most reptiles live in warm parts of the world.

Diplodocus was a dinosaur that lived on Earth millions of years ago.

Scientists divide reptiles into four groups—snakes and lizards, turtles and tortoises, crocodilians, and tuataras. Why are snakes and lizards in the same group? They may look different, but they have a lot in common. Most have little teeth that grow right out of their jawbones. They have a special way of finding food and sensing danger. When one of these animals presses the tip of its tongue against

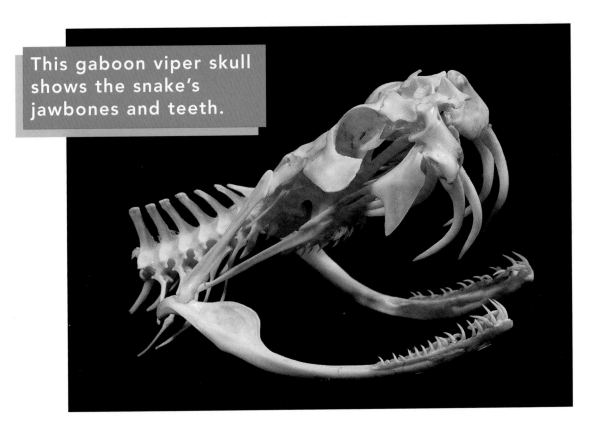

the roof of its mouth, its Jacobson's organ sends a message to the animal's brain. Within seconds, the snake or lizard knows if a meal—or trouble—is near.

A Look at Lizards

Lizards live on every continent except Antarctica. They live in trees, in the ocean, and on the ground. They glide through the air, scamper up walls, scoot upside down along ceilings, and even walk on water.

A lizard's legs and feet can give you clues about where it

A basilisk lizard can walk across water.

lives. Some desert lizards have long scales on their toes and can walk easily in soft sand. Tree-climbing lizards live in forests and use their sharp claws to grip tree branches. The webbed feet of marine iguanas make them good swimmers. Burrowing lizards spend most of their time underground. They have no legs at all.

Lizards have different ways of avoiding their enemies. Some lizards are excellent runners. They scurry out of sight when they sense danger. Other lizards face their enemies.

A frilled lizard can make itself look very scary. A gila monster's bright colors warn predators to stay away.

Many slower lizards have colors that match their surround- ings. When a predator comes near, they stay perfectly still and wait for it to go away. An anole lizard blends in with leaves. A

The green anole blends in with its leafy surroundings.

spade-tailed gecko is hard to spot when it rests on the bark of a tree.

Other lizards have a special trick. If a predator grabs them by the tail, they drop their tail and run away.

This gold dust day gecko has just dropped its tail.

Turtles and Tortoises

Turtles are different from other reptiles because part of their skeleton surrounds their body. We call this hard outer covering a shell. Turtles live in fields, forests, deserts, swamps, the ocean, ponds, lakes, and rivers.

You can tell where a turtle lives by looking at its feet.

Like most sea turtles, the hawksbill turtle has flippers. It also has an unusual parrotlike beak.

Turtles that spend time in ponds, lakes, and rivers have toes with claws. Sometimes they have webbing between their toes. Turtles that spend most of their time in the ocean have flippers. Turtles that spend all their time on land are called tortoises. The toes of these turtles are fused together, so that their feet look some-thing like an elephant's feet.

Desert tortoises blend in with their surroundings, and they usually live a long time.

A box turtle lays its eggs, which will hatch in the fall.

Almost all turtles lay eggs on land. Some land turtles can live for more than 100 years.

Slithering Snakes

Almost everyone has seen a snake. Most snakes have long, thin bodies and no legs. There are about 2,700 kinds of snakes living on Earth, but only about 200 of them are venomous.

Some kinds of snakes wrap their bodies around an animal

This yellow anaconda
has caught a caiman.

until it cannot breathe and
dies. These snakes are called
constrictors. Some snakes can
eat very large prey. The egg-
eating snake can unhinge its
jaws to fit large eggs inside.

Other snakes use the same method to eat gazelle or pigs. Snakes digest their food very slowly and can go weeks between meals.

To move, a snake uses the wide overlapping scales on its belly. The back edges of these scales catch and hold on to the ground as muscles inside the snake push it forward. A snake's backbone is made up of hundreds of small bones, so it is very flexible.

This corn snake is laying eggs.

Most snakes lay eggs in a nest or hole. Only a few kinds of snakes take care of their eggs. Male and female cobras take turns guarding their nests. Most snake eggs hatch after about 2 months. Young snakes are ready to survive on their own as soon as they hatch.

Some snakes do not lay eggs. Young Costa Rican hog-nosed vipers grow inside their mother's body. When

The Costa Rican hog-nosed viper is a venomous snake. Its young grow inside the female until they are fully developed.

the young are ready to be born, their mother pushes them out of her body. Some kinds of lizards give birth in the same way.

Crocodiles and Their Relatives

Many scientists believe that the crocodilians are the closest living relatives of the dinosaurs. This group includes crocodiles, alligators, gavials, and caimans. These animals have long bodies, flat heads, and strong tails. Their powerful jaws have rows of long, sharp teeth. They live in and around swamps, lakes, and rivers in warm areas of the world.

The best way to tell the difference between a crocodile and its relatives is by looking at the snout. A crocodile has a pointed snout. An alligator has a broad, rounded snout. A caiman's snout looks like an alligator's, but it is shorter. A gavial's snout is very long and thin.

Compare the snouts of the American alligator (top right), Nile crocodile (above), smooth-fronted caiman (right), and gavial (below).

This alligator has covered its nest and is guarding it.

A female crocodilian builds a large nest on land and lays her eggs. Then she covers the nest to keep the eggs warm. She usually guards the nest to protect the eggs from predators. When she hears the young grunting inside their eggs, she uncovers her nest.

Sometimes the young run straight to the water. In other cases, the mother carries them to the water in her

These American alligator young are resting safely on their mother's head.

mouth. She stays close by until the young are a few weeks old. For their first few weeks or months, young crocodilians eat insects, worms, and small fish. As they grow, they eat larger animals, such as lizards and rats. Adults can eat animals as large as antelope, zebras, cows, or even people.

Tales of

The word "tuatara" means "peaks on the back." This lizard-like animal has a crest running down its back and tail. It also has a third eye on the top of its head. The eye cannot see objects, but it can sense light.

Tuataras live on a few small islands near New Zealand. During the day, they rest in

It is difficult to see the tuatara's third eye because scales cover it.

Tuataras

underground burrows. At night, they hunt for insects, spiders, earthworms, slugs, snails, geckos, baby birds, and birds' eggs.

Tuataras grow very slowly. They cannot have young until they are 20 years old, and may not be full-grown until they are 50 years old. They may live more than 100 years.

A young tuatara

Reptiles in Our Lives

Reptiles play an important role in our lives. In some parts of the world, people eat the meat of turtles and alligators. Lizards and snakes eat insects and small mammals, such as rats and mice, that harm crops.

As we clear land to build homes, roads, and shopping

This corn snake is eating a mouse that might have eaten this corn crop.

These bags were made from crocodile skins.

centers, we destroy the homes of many reptiles. Other reptiles are killed so that we can make belts, shoes, and other leather products from their skins. As a result, many reptiles are now in danger of disappearing from Earth forever. We must do whatever we can to make sure that reptiles continue to live in our world.

To Find Out More

Here are some additional resources to help you learn more about reptiles:

 **Books**

Berger, Melvin. **Look Out for Turtles.** HarperCollins, 1992.

Conant, Roger. **Peterson's First Guide to Reptiles and Amphibians.** Houghton Mifflin, 1992.

Howell, Catherine Herbert. **Reptiles and Amphibians.** National Geographic Society, 1993.

Landau, Elaine. **Your Pet Iguana.** Children's Press, 1997.

Lovett, Sarah. **Extremely Weird Reptiles.** John Muir Publications, 1996.

Miller, Sara Swan. **Turtles.** Franklin Watts, 1999.

_____. **Snakes and Lizards.** Franklin Watts, 2000.

Snedden, Robert. **What Is a Reptile?** Sierra Club Books, 1995.

Anatomy of a Snake
*http://herpetology.com/
anatomy.html*

This site features a labeled diagram of a snake's body parts.

Birmingham Zoo: Alligators
*http://www.birminghamzoo.
com/animals/gator.html*

To find out more about American alligators, check out this site. It features photos and information about what they eat, where they live, and how they are different from crocodiles.

Crocodilians: Natural History & Conservation
http://crocodilian.com/

Whether you're interested in crocodiles, alligators, gavials, or caimans, this site has the information you want. You can learn all about the twenty-three kinds of crocodilians, take a peek at the crocodilian of the month, listen to crocodiles calling, and more.

Gecko Land
*http://netterra.com/
geckoland/*

This site answers all your questions about geckos and how to care for them.

Kingsnake & Milk Snake Page
*http://www.kingsnake.com/
king/*

Learn all about these snakes, and see photographs of them. This site includes instructions for caring for snakes in the genus *Lampropeltis.*

Turtle, Sea Turtle, and Tortoise
*http://www.xmission.com/
~gastown/herpmed/
chelonia.htm*

This site includes turtle trivia, specific information about some turtles, as well as links to sites that describe conservation efforts, how to build a turtle pond, and more.

45

Important Words

cold blooded having a body temperature that changes as air or water temperature changes

constrictor a snake that kills its prey by squeezing it until it cannot breathe and dies

crocodilian a member of the group of reptiles that includes crocodiles, alligators, gavials, and caimans

Jacobson's organ a sense organ on the roof of a snake or lizard's mouth

predator an animal that kills and eats other animals

snout the long front part of the head of an animal that projects outward

tuatara a lizard-like reptile that lives on a few small islands near New Zealand

venomous having a gland that produces poison

Index

Meet the Author

Melissa Stewart earned a Bachelor's Degree in biology from Union College and a Master's Degree in Science and Environmental Journalism from New York University. She has been writing about science and nature for almost a decade. Ms. Stewart lives in Danbury, Connecticut.